Joseph E. Johnston

Confederate General

Colonial Leaders

Lord Baltimore
English Politician and Colonist

Benjamin Banneker
American Mathematician and Astronomer

Sir William Berkeley
Governor of Virginia

William Bradford
Governor of Plymouth Colony

Jonathan Edwards
Colonial Religious Leader

Benjamin Franklin
American Statesman, Scientist, and Writer

Anne Hutchinson
Religious Leader

Cotton Mather
Author, Clergyman, and Scholar

Increase Mather
Clergyman and Scholar

James Oglethorpe
Humanitarian and Soldier

William Penn
Founder of Democracy

Sir Walter Raleigh
English Explorer and Author

Caesar Rodney
American Patriot

John Smith
English Explorer and Colonist

Miles Standish
Plymouth Colony Leader

Peter Stuyvesant
Dutch Military Leader

George Whitefield
Clergyman and Scholar

Roger Williams
Founder of Rhode Island

John Winthrop
Politician and Statesman

John Peter Zenger
Free Press Advocate

Revolutionary War Leaders

John Adams
Second U.S. President

Samuel Adams
Patriot

Ethan Allen
Revolutionary Hero

Benedict Arnold
Traitor to the Cause

John Burgoyne
British General

George Rogers Clark
American General

Lord Cornwallis
British General

Thomas Gage
British General

King George III
English Monarch

Nathanael Greene
Military Leader

Nathan Hale
Revolutionary Hero

Alexander Hamilton
First U.S. Secretary of the Treasury

John Hancock
President of the Continental Congress

Patrick Henry
American Statesman and Speaker

William Howe
British General

John Jay
First Chief Justice of the Supreme Court

Thomas Jefferson
Author of the Declaration of Independence

John Paul Jones
Father of the U.S. Navy

Thaddeus Kosciuszko
Polish General and Patriot

Lafayette
French Freedom Fighter

James Madison
Father of the Constitution

Francis Marion
The Swamp Fox

James Monroe
American Statesman

Thomas Paine
Political Writer

Molly Pitcher
Heroine

Paul Revere
American Patriot

Betsy Ross
American Patriot

Baron Von Steuben
American General

George Washington
First U.S. President

Anthony Wayne
American General

Famous Figures of the Civil War Era

John Brown
Abolitionist

Jefferson Davis
Confederate President

Frederick Douglass
Abolitionist and Author

Stephen A. Douglas
Champion of the Union

David Farragut
Union Admiral

Ulysses S. Grant
Military Leader and President

Stonewall Jackson
Confederate General

Joseph E. Johnston
Confederate General

Robert E. Lee
Confederate General

Abraham Lincoln
Civil War President

George Gordon Meade
Union General

George McClellan
Union General

William Henry Seward
Senator and Statesman

Philip Sheridan
Union General

William Sherman
Union General

Edwin Stanton
Secretary of War

Harriet Beecher Stowe
Author of Uncle Tom's Cabin

James Ewell Brown Stuart
Confederate General

Sojourner Truth
Abolitionist, Suffragist, and Preacher

Harriet Tubman
Leader of the Underground Railroad

Joseph E. Johnston

Confederate General

Christin Ditchfield

Arthur M. Schlesinger, jr.
Senior Consulting Editor

Chelsea House Publishers

Philadelphia

CHELSEA HOUSE PUBLISHERS
Editor-in-Chief Sally Cheney
Director of Production Kim Shinners
Production Manager Pamela Loos
Art Director Sara Davis
Production Editor Diann Grasse

Staff for JOSEPH E. JOHNSTON
Editor Sally Cheney
Associate Art Director Takeshi Takahashi
Series Design Keith Trego
Layout by D&G Limited, LLC

The Chelsea House World Wide Web address is
http://www.chelseahouse.com

First Printing
1 3 5 7 9 8 6 4 2

Library of Congress Cataloging-in-Publication Data

Ditchfield, Christin.
    Joseph E. Johnston : Confederate general / Christin Ditchfield.
      p. cm. — (Famous figures of the Civil War era)
    Includes bibliographical references and index.
    ISBN 0-7910-6412-3 (alk. paper) — ISBN 0-7910-6413-1 (pbk. :
    alk. paper)
      1. Johnston, Joseph E. (Joseph Eggleston), 1807-1891—Juvenile
    literature. 2. Generals—Confederate States of America—
    Biography—Juvenile literature. 3. Confederate States of America.
    Army—Biography—Juvenile literature. 4. United States—History—
    Civil War, 1861-1865—Campaigns—Juvenile literature.
    [1. Johnston, Joseph E. (Joseph Eggleston), 1807-1891.
    2. Generals. 3. United States—History—Civil War, 1861-1865.]
    I. Title. II. Series.

    E467.1.J74 D58 2001
    973.7'3'092—dc21
    [B]   2001028765

Contents

Patrick Henry is shown here addressing the Virginia Assembly in 1765. This respected political leader of the American Revolution was Joseph's great uncle.

1

A Family Tradition

Over 150 years ago, America began its tragic **Civil War.** General Joseph E. Johnston was the highest-ranking officer in the U.S. Army to resign from his position and join the Confederate forces in the South. He led the Southern armies to their first victory at Manassas (also known as the First Battle of Bull Run) in 1861. He also led them to their *last* victory, at Bentonville, North Carolina, in 1865. All through the war, General Johnston served his country proudly.

From the very beginning, it seemed that he was born to be a soldier.

On February 3, 1807, in Farmville, Virginia, Peter and Mary Johnston welcomed their seventh son into their family. Peter had been a lieutenant in the Revolutionary War. He named the little boy after his old squad commander, Joseph Eggleston. Mary's uncle, Patrick Henry, was one of the great political leaders of the American Revolution. Many members of the family had held military or government positions. They believed in patriotism and service to their country. It was a Johnston family tradition!

When Joseph Eggleston Johnston was four years old, his father became a judge in the state's General Court. The Johnstons moved to Abingdon, a small **frontier** town in the mountains of Virginia. Abingdon lay close to the border of Tennessee–yet more than 300 miles from the nearest city. Joe and his brothers spent hours exploring the outdoors. They learned to ride and hunt. They hiked in the mountains and swam in the streams. But more than anything else, Joe loved to play war games. He got his brothers and his friends to help him act out the Battle of King's Mountain. He talked with all the older men in town, most of whom were Revolutionary War veterans. Joe listened eagerly to their battle stories, over and over again. He dreamed that one day he, too, would be a soldier.

Peter noticed his young son's interest in the military. Although he had six older sons, Peter decided to give eight-year-old Joe a very special gift: the sword that he himself had worn into battle. Joe treasured that sword for as long as he lived.

Life wasn't all wilderness fun and games for the Johnston boys. Mr. and Mrs. Johnston wanted every one of their sons to

Joe Johnston and his brothers often went horseback riding through the mountains of Virginia. On one ride, Joe was thrown from his horse and broke his leg in the fall. One of the bones pierced through his skin. But Joe didn't scream or cry. He calmly called the other boys to come and see what had happened to him. His brothers carried him on their shoulders to the nearest doctor, who lived miles away. Throughout the trip, Joe never cried out in pain. Like the war heroes he admired, Joe showed great courage and bravery in times of trouble.

be properly educated. They sent Joe and all of his brothers to the Abingdon Academy. His teachers noted that Joe was a hardworking and obedient student. Joe had a reason for wanting to do well: He knew he needed good grades to get into the military academy.

All of his hard work paid off. In 1825, at age 18, Joe was ready to take the next step in his dream of becoming a soldier. He enrolled in the United States Military Academy at West Point to begin his training. If Joe thought the Abingdon Academy was tough, he found his new school even more challenging. Every day, he and the other **cadets** practiced marches and field drills for four hours at a time. Joe studied engineering– learning how to build forts, bridges, tunnels, and railroads. He struggled in his math and science classes. But he got high marks in battle **tactics** and **strategy**. All West Point students were required to learn French so that they could learn from the writings of General Napoleon Bonaparte. Napoleon had been the Emperor of France and

Joseph's decision to go to West Point would later lead to his command of Confederate troops. These Southern soldiers from Louisiana posed for photographer J. W. Petty.

was widely recognized as one of the greatest military leaders in history. French turned out to be Joe's best subject. He quickly learned to speak the language well. He began reading French books on engineering, military skills, and war heroes. He even translated some of them into English.

As before, Joe took his schoolwork seriously, and he was determined to do his best. His grades improved every year. Unlike many of his fellow students, Joe tried hard to stay out of trouble. He carefully followed the school rules and rarely ever received a **demerit**. Some of the other cadets nicknamed Joe "The Colonel," because he was so quiet and serious and proper. But to Joe, becoming a soldier was the most important thing in his life. He didn't want anything to get in the way of his dream.

At West Point, Joe found a friend who shared his feelings. Like Joe, Robert E. Lee was born in Virginia, to a military family. In fact, Joe's father had served under Robert's father–"Light-Horse Harry" Lee–in the American Revolution. Both young men were good students and wanted to become great soldiers like their fathers. Neither one wasted time by getting into mischief. Joe and Robert soon became best friends. They were also **rivals**, as they competed for the honors of their class at West Point. Somehow, Robert always came in just ahead of Joe in the competition. When they graduated from West Point in 1829, Robert E. Lee ranked second out of the 46 students in the class. Joe was ranked 13th.

Joseph Johnston became friends with Robert E. Lee while they were both at West Point. Lee was a skilled military leader in the U.S. Army before he joined the South as a general in the Civil War.

After graduation on July 1, 1829, Joe Johnston's lifelong dream came true: He was appointed as an officer in the **artillery** division of the U.S. Army. It would be a long time before he experienced his first battle action.

Johnston was an aide to General Winfield Scott during the Seminole Wars, which were fought in Florida.

Restless Years

Second Lieutenant Joseph E. Johnston was proud to be an officer of the United States Army. For two years, he served at Fort Columbus in New York. It wasn't exactly an exciting life. During the day, he took classes to learn more about the guns and weapons of the artillery division. At night, he and his friend Robert E. Lee talked with the other officers or went out to dinner parties and dances. Joe wrote letters to his family, telling them how bored he was. He longed for action and adventure. In the spring of 1832, it looked like Joe would get his wish.

The U.S. Army was fighting a war against many American Indian tribes. A few years earlier, President Andrew Jackson had forced Indian chiefs to

Black Hawk was born in 1767. His father and grandfather had both been war chiefs, and Black Hawk followed in their footsteps. The brave warrior did not trust the white people. He felt that they had treated the Native Americans badly. The Black Hawk War started when the courageous chief refused to obey the U.S. Army and leave his tribal lands. After his capture, Black Hawk became one of the most famous Native American leaders in history. He **dictated** his life story to an interpreter. It was the first Native American autobiography ever published in America. Chief Black Hawk died in 1838.

sign an unfair **treaty**. This treaty stated that all American Indians who lived in the eastern states would have to move west across the Mississippi River—and away from white settlers. When Chief Black Hawk returned to the east, the army set out to capture him and his men. Joe Johnston's unit was called in to help. Joe thought he would finally see some battle action. But the trip turned out to be a disaster for Joe and his men.

To join the rest of the army, they traveled mostly by river—a journey of over 1,000 miles. Joe was seasick much of the time. The ships were small and crowded. Some of the soldiers caught a disease called Asiatic

The Native Americans and the settlers often fought over the rights to ownership of land.

cholera. It quickly spread from one person to another. By the time the ships arrived at their destination, more than half of the men in Joe's command had died. Of the 850 men who started the trip, only 200 were healthy enough to carry out their duties. When they reached Fort Armstrong, they learned that the Black Hawk War was already over. Chief Black Hawk had been captured. There was nothing for the soldiers to do. They turned around and headed home.

Some time later, Joe received a special assignment. He worked as an aide to General Winfield Scott in 1835, during the Florida Seminole War. Again, he hoped for excitement and adventure. Once again, he was disappointed. Many times over the next few years, Joe would be sent into conflicts with the Native Americans—with little or no result. It seemed to Joe that it was always a waste of time and effort. The senior officers spent most of their time arguing with each other over who was in charge. There were many mix-ups and mistakes. The pay was low; the work was dull. No one ever accomplished anything.

In eight years, Joe never got a chance to command troops in combat. He felt that all his work at West Point had been useless. His frustration grew and grew, and on May 31, 1837, he resigned from the army.

Joe thought he could make a lot more money—and have more success—as an engineer. Unfortunately, he chose a bad time to start his new career. Financial problems had shut down

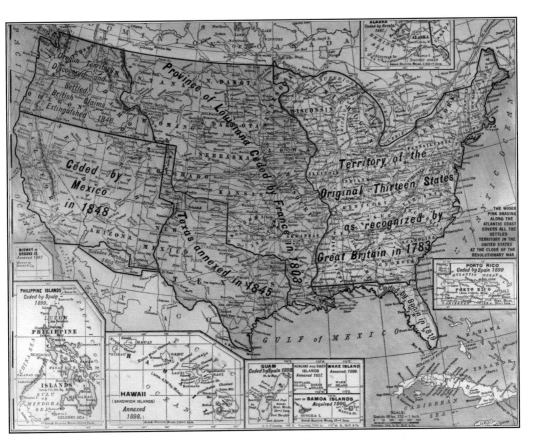

This map shows how the United States looked in the 1800s. Joe resigned from the army in 1837 and took a job with the government's Topographical Bureau. He surveyed areas and made detailed maps of possible sites for forts.

many banks and businesses. Construction of new bridges, canals, and railroads had stopped. When he couldn't find work in engineering, Joe took a job with the government's **Topographical** Bureau. He thought he would be working in an office, designing maps and filling out official papers.

Instead, his new job took him into the swamps. He traveled with a team of Navy officers who were exploring the Florida coast. Joe surveyed the area, made detailed maps, and helped pick out good sites for future forts. Although he wasn't in the army anymore, Joe had more military experience and training than any of the officers or soldiers on the team. That experience came in handy more than once.

Several times, Seminole Indians attacked the exploration party. In one attack, a bullet grazed Joe's head. He wasn't badly hurt, but he did have a permanent scar. Another attack turned out to be deadly. As the officers in the party were wounded, Joe quickly took command. Because of his military training, he knew just what to do. In spite of the confusion of the battle, Joe was calm and in control. His quick thinking spared many lives that day. Later, the soldiers praised him for his courage and bravery. The officers wrote a special report of the battle and gave Joe the credit for saving the day. Otherwise, they said, the whole event would have been a tragedy and a disaster. Adventure, excitement, the chance to be a hero–this was just what Joe had longed for all of those years in the army.

Joe was so encouraged by his experience in Florida that he decided to return to the army. He became a first lieutenant in the new Corps of Topographical Engineers. Things were looking up for Joe.

In 1840, Joe spent Christmas in Baltimore, Maryland, with the family of his friend, Second Lieutenant Robert McLane. Robert's father, Louis, was a wealthy and powerful man. Louis had served in both the House of Representatives and the United States Senate. At one time or another, he had been the United States Ambassador to England, Secretary of the Treasury, and Secretary of State. Many people thought he would run for president. Louis McLane liked Joe immediately and welcomed him into the family circle. Joe enjoyed his friendship with the McLanes and visited them often. He especially liked spending time with Lydia, their beautiful dark-haired, dark-eyed daughter. Lydia was warm and sweet and friendly. Although Joe was 15 years older than Lydia, the two soon became best friends. Eventually their affection grew into love.

For five years, Joe and Lydia kept in touch through long letters and brief visits. Joe's army career kept him busy. He had been promoted to assistant adjutant general. Finally, on July 10, 1845, Joe and Lydia were married in Baltimore. Joe was 38; Lydia was 23. The two sweethearts shared a deep and lasting love for one another. Lydia had many health problems, and Joe and Lydia never had any children. Joe faced serious challenges in his career. Through good times and bad, the Johnstons encouraged and supported each other.

Soon after Joe and Lydia were married, war broke out between the United States and Mexico. The two countries fought over which one of them owned the land in Texas. Joe saw the war as a great opportunity to be the soldier he had always wanted to be. He could fight in real battles, develop his military skills, and earn the promotion and glory he had dreamed of since childhood.

For once, things went exactly as Joe hoped they would. Over and over on the battlefield, he proved his steadiness, bravery, and leadership ability. In one ambush, he was badly wounded. For his courage, Joe received a double promotion to lieutenant colonel. He recovered from his injury in time to lead the U.S. Army to its most decisive victory of the war, the capture of Mexico City. Joe was injured twice more–but he didn't mind. He was proud of his battle scars and proud of his service to his country.

In the years after the war, Joe finally got the rank and honor he had desperately wanted in

United States General Winfield Scott and his men entered Mexico City and won the last battle of the Mexican-American War. At the end of the war, the Treaty of Guadalupe Hidalgo set the southern boundary of Texas and gave New Mexico and California to the United States.

his army career. In 1860 he even became the first West Point graduate to be promoted to brigadier general. The Secretary of War appointed Joe to serve as quartermaster general. He would be in charge of ordering and providing supplies for the entire United States Army.

For this new job, Joe and Lydia moved to the nation's capital, Washington, D.C. Joe couldn't have been happier. He had proved himself in combat. He had achieved the success he always wanted. Now he was ready to settle down. He looked forward to working in an office and leading a quieter life, but things wouldn't stay quiet for long.

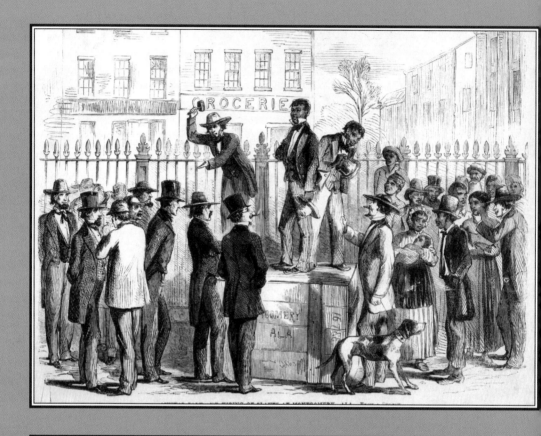

Men, women, and children were taken from Africa and brought to the United States. They were then sold to plantation owners in the South. Slaves worked for little or no money in the fields and homes of their owners, and they had no rights or freedoms. This arrangement benefited the plantation owners and was an important part of the Southern economy. Plantation owners could operate their farms with very few expenses.

3

Fighting Fury

While Joe Johnston steadily moved up the ranks in the U. S. Army, trouble was brewing across the country. Sharp disagreements arose between the Northern and Southern states. One cause of disagreement was **slavery**. For hundreds of years, African people had been kidnapped from their homes, brought to America, and sold as slaves. They were forced to work for the people who bought them. In the South, farmers grew large quantities of cotton and other crops. They depended on slave labor to help them run their vast **plantations**. In the Northern states, more people worked in factories than on farms. They did not have the same need for labor. Many people in the North believed that

Abraham Lincoln was elected as the 16th president of the United States in November 1860. The Southern states did not like Lincoln's policies on slavery. Before his inauguration in March 1861, Southern states had already started to secede from the Union. This 1864 portrait of Lincoln was taken by photographer Mathew Brady.

slavery was wrong. They decided to make slavery illegal in their states, and they tried to force the Southern states to do the same.

Not everyone in the South was in favor of slavery. But many believed in "states' rights"–that each state had the right to make its own laws. They believed that the national government should not make decisions for them and should not make laws without each state's approval. The Southern states grew angry at the national government. They felt that the government made laws that treated them unfairly. In 1860, South Carolina announced that it would **secede** from the country. It would no longer be a part of the United States of America.

The Northern states insisted that South Carolina did not have the right to secede. They wanted the president to send armies to South Carolina to take control of the state. South Carolina wanted the rest of the Southern states to join it in forming a new country, the **Confederate States of America**. Some people started talking about war between the North and the South.

At first, Joe Johnston hoped that there would be a peaceful resolution to the crisis. As the highest-ranking officer in the army, he felt a deep sense of loyalty to the U.S. government. For 35 years, he had proudly served his country and its armed forces. He did not particularly believe in slavery and he thought that South Carolina's decision to secede from the **Union** was probably illegal. But his deepest loyalty belonged to his home state, Virginia. Joe told his friends that if Virginia remained in the Union, he would remain. If Virginia joined the Confederate states, he would, too.

On April 17, 1861, Virginia officially seceded from the United States. A few days later, Joe Johnston walked to his office in the War Department and turned in his resignation. With tears in his eyes, he explained, "I must go with the South."

The next day, Joe and Lydia left their home in Washington. They traveled to the Confederate

Shown here is Richmond, Virginia, which was the capital of the Confederacy.

headquarters in Richmond, Virginia. Joe brought with him his pistols and his father's Revolutionary War sword. In Virginia, Joe met with leaders of the new Confederate States of America. He spoke to Confederate President Jefferson Davis and with his old friend Robert E. Lee. Lee had just joined the Confederates a few days earlier. Joe agreed to help the Confederate states organize an army.

When Joe arrived to take his command at Harpers Ferry, Virginia, he found that the men were disorganized and undisciplined. They had little food and few weapons. More than a third of the men were sick with the mumps or measles. Joe realized he had a big job ahead of him, if he was going to turn these volunteers into battle-ready troops. The men observed their new commander with great interest. Now 54, General Johnston's hair and beard were white. His deep brown eyes sparkled with warmth and intelligence. Although he was not very tall, he stood straight and carried himself with authority. He kept himself and his uniform in perfect condition. Joe's quiet confidence inspired his men to trust him and follow his lead.

As Joe began to train his troops, he wrote many letters to President Davis and General Lee asking them for more supplies and more men. This was a request that they were often unable to fulfill. Joe wanted to know exactly what was expected of him. He grew concerned when it appeared to him that Davis and Lee didn't have any clear direction.

On July 21, 1861, the first major battle of the Civil War took place at Manassas—also called Bull Run. Under the command of General McDowell, the Union forces attacked the Confederate forces of General P.G.T. Beauregard.

Throughout the war, Joe insisted that the best battle strategy could be found in "concentration of force." He felt that to defeat the more powerful forces of the Union, the Confederates needed to combine their armies and concentrate their attacks in specific areas. Joe always wanted more men—it was one of the reasons he rarely attacked his opponents. Unfortunately, the Confederate armies were usually outnumbered. Other officers didn't always agree with Joe's strategy. And in any case, they rarely ever had any extra troops they could send him. It didn't stop Joe from asking over and over again.

General Joe Johnston and his men came to Beauregard's defense. At the scene of the battle,

The first major battle of the Civil War took place on July 21, 1861, at Manassas Junction on the Bull Run River in Virginia.

there was great confusion and disorder. Joe quickly took command. While Beauregard rode up and down shouting encouragement to the troops, Joe started coordinating the attack. He rearranged the position of the different

regiments and directed the commanders as they moved into place. At times, he led them into combat. At the end of the day, Joe's men had held their ground. Fresh **reinforcements** arrived just in time, and the weary Union forces fled.

This was Joe's first triumph as an army commander, and he deserved the credit for his cool and steady direction in the heat of battle. Unfortunately, General Beauregard seemed to get all the glory. It irritated Joe that Beauregard got so much attention, especially since he had not been much help in the battle. This was only the first of many such disappointments for Joe.

For the next few months, the Confederate forces camped out in Virginia and prepared for winter. It was during this time that Joe began his bitter, lifelong feud with Confederate President Jefferson Davis. The Confederate government had passed a law allowing the president to name five men as full generals in the Confederate army. The law stated that the rank of officers

In 1861, Jefferson Davis was elected president of the Confederate States of America, which was made up of the proslavery Southern states. Davis and Johnston disagreed on battle strategy and carried on a life-long feud after the war was over.

would be directly related to the previous positions they had held in the U.S. Army. As a former brigadier general, Joe outranked all of the other officers. Joe thought he would be given the highest position in the Confederate forces. But when Davis named the new generals, he gave them all equal rank. Joe wasn't even put first on the list, instead he was fourth, after Robert E. Lee. Joe was deeply hurt and offended. He wrote a long letter to Davis complaining of the "injustice" of his actions. He even accused him of breaking the law.

President Davis was angry about the letter. Throughout the war and for the rest of their lives, the two men argued about everything that happened between them. They criticized each other publicly to their friends, to the newspapers, and to anybody who would listen. And they never forgave each other.

For the rest of the war, the two men argued over decisions, disagreed on strategy, and questioned each other's judgment. Joe felt that he could no longer trust President Davis. Joe believed that President Davis interfered with his command and made foolish decisions. Although he never directly disobeyed Davis's orders, Joe sometimes delayed putting them into action. Whenever possible, he acted without telling President Davis, to avoid any further interference. Robert E. Lee sympathized with him because he was Joe's old friend and classmate. But Lee could also see Davis's side. He tried to be a peacemaker between two men. It was a tough job.

As the war went on, Joe frequently evacuated his troops before they could be attacked. President Davis complained that he was too quick to retreat. But Joe was cautious and never sent his troops into an attack if they weren't prepared to win. For weeks, Joe had retreated from General McClellan's forces back and forth over the Virginia peninsula. Then on May 31, 1862, Joe saw an opportunity to attack the Union forces at Seven Pines, also called Fair Oaks. Joe had a

Forces under Union General George McClellan, pictured here, fought the Confederates at the Battle of Fair Oaks (also called Seven Pines). Joe was seriously wounded during the fighting.

simple plan: he would divide up his regiments and have them approach the Northern army at Seven Pines from several different angles. Unfortunately, he didn't do a good job of communicating the plan to his commanders, and several men misunderstood their orders. Others made changes without consulting Joe. In the confusion that followed, nothing went as planned. Joe went to the front lines to try to straighten things out. As he rode up and down the lines, a bullet struck him in the shoulder. A few seconds later, he was hit in the chest. He fell off of his horse, unconscious. Joe's men carried him off the field. As he came to, he asked for his father's sword. When he was told that it had been left on the battlefield, Joe sent a soldier to get it for him. He couldn't rest until it had been found.

Joe had been seriously wounded. It would take him six months to recover. Robert E. Lee took command of the Confederate forces. He led them to several decisive victories, demonstrating incredible leadership and military skill. Lee became the hero of the South. Joe could only watch, and wait for his wounds to heal.

Confederate soldiers are shown resting at their camp between battles.

Retreating Joe

Joe wanted to get back to the battlefield. He hated sitting on the sidelines as the war raged on. While he recovered from his injuries, Joe spent a lot of time talking to leaders of the Confederacy. He complained bitterly about the treatment he had received from President Jefferson Davis. Joe blamed the mistakes that the South had made in battle on Davis's interference. More and more politicians had started to dislike President Davis. They agreed with Joe and supported him in any way that they could. Whenever there were arguments or controversies over army leadership, Texas Senator Louis T. Wigfall came to Joe's defense. Unfortunately, this only added to the problems between Joe and President Davis. Wigfall and Davis were fierce enemies. Senator Wigfall made no secret of his dislike for Davis. Jefferson Davis looked at Joe's friendship with the senator as an act of treason.

Joe had almost fully recovered by the fall of 1862. He was ready to return to his command in Virginia. But Jefferson Davis had no intention of removing Robert E. Lee, after his enormously successful campaigns. Instead, he assigned Joe to the "Department of the West"—a large territory between the Appalachian Mountains and the Mississippi River. Davis explained that he wanted Joe to organize this new department and explore different strategies for defeating the Union forces in the west. It wasn't what he wanted, but Joe accepted the assignment. In November 1863 he traveled to Chattanooga, Tennessee, to set up his headquarters.

Joe saw at once that Davis had made a big mistake with the Department of the West. The area he had sent Joe to command was huge. Four separate Confederate armies operated independently in the area. None of the commanders worked well together. Under the circumstances, it was hard to communicate and coordinate strategy. Joe repeatedly wrote to Jefferson Davis with complaints, suggestions, and requests for more supplies and support. Joe resented being put in a position where he could not succeed. Joe's battle wounds had not completely healed. They were aggravated by the constant travel of his new job. Joe was ill for quite some time.

After five months in the west, Joe got orders to move his troops east. General Braxton Bragg and General John C. Pemberton needed help defending the city of Vicksburg in Mississippi. Joe sent them advice and directions, but he refused to get personally involved. He brought his troops near the city, but never attempted to enter it. Although President Davis had asked him to take charge, Joe did not want the responsibility. He disagreed with the strategy and methods of the other commanders and believed that their efforts were doomed to fail. Consequently, he delayed his response to

This photograph from 1863 shows Union army dugout on a hillside near Vicksburg, Mississippi.

Davis's request. In the end, the Confederate forces lost the Battle of Vicksburg and surrendered in July 1863. President Davis, General Pemberton, and several other officers blamed Joe.

As a result, Davis reduced Joe's command to a much smaller post in Mississippi. Joe might have been stationed there for the rest of the war, if it hadn't been for General Bragg. President Davis had to replace Bragg because of the terrible job he was doing with his troops. After the Army of Virginia, the Army of Tennessee was the second most important army in the Confederacy. Davis came under pressure from Joe's supporters in Congress to appoint the general as Tennessee's new commander. After some time, Davis reluctantly agreed.

When Joe arrived at the camp, in December 1863, the soldiers cheered wildly. They had suffered through a series of awful commanders who spent more time drinking and fighting with each other than leading their troops. The camp was in a state of disrepair and many of the soldiers had gone hungry and barefoot. They were excited to be put under the command of a general with Joe's solid reputation. Joe set a new tone in the Army of Tennessee. He immediately ordered the shoes, clothes, and supplies for the soldiers. He had new tents and buildings constructed. He came up with a rotating system that allowed the soldiers to go on **furlough** to rest and visit with their families. The soldiers of the Army of Tennessee could feel

Union General William Tecumseh Sherman marched across Georgia and headed to Atlanta, leaving a path of destroyed railroads, bridges, homes, and crops.

Joe's genuine concern for them. They became fiercely loyal to their new general and praised and admired him.

In May 1864, Union General William Tecumseh Sherman began a march across Georgia.

Sherman was a tough and determined soldier. As he moved through the South, he ordered his troops to destroy railroads and bridges, burn homes and hospitals, and trample crops. Sherman headed for the city of Atlanta, leaving a wide path of destruction everywhere he went. Joe and the Army of Tennessee stood in his way. Sherman's army was at least twice the size of Joe's. Joe did not have the men or supplies necessary to attack Sherman head on, so he relied on strategy instead.

Once Joe came across some of his soldiers struggling to move a huge gun that was stuck in the mud. Weary and discouraged, they admitted that they would probably have to abandon the gun. "Oh, no!" Joe said, "I reckon not! Let me see what I can do." The general jumped off his horse, waded into the knee-deep mud, and started pulling. The soldiers were stunned. After a moment, they joined him, and together they got the gun free. Joe may have had problems with his superior officers. But with his enlisted men, he was always kind and considerate—quick to offer assistance. They respected him for it.

For more than 70 days, the two armies were in constant contact with one another. As the Union soldiers advanced, Joe and his men defended

A Union officer (seated) is surrounded by his men at their camp.

their territory. Time and time again, they skillfully evaded capture. And although they were being forced to retreat, they made Sherman win every single inch he took. Joe tried to attack whenever he had the advantage. He did not defeat Sherman, but he kept him from taking Atlanta.

For some people in the South–including President Davis–this was not enough. They were angry at Joe's lack of progress against Sherman.

Some had nicknamed the mild-mannered general "Retreating Joe." They accused him of being a coward and said he was afraid to fight. But Joe was not afraid to fight. He was afraid to fail. He came from a family with a great military tradition, and Joe prized his reputation more than anything. He was more afraid of making an embarrassing mistake than of taking a bullet in the service of his country. Joe's fear of failure kept him from taking risks. Sometimes it kept him from achieving the honor and success he desired.

People in the South wanted a quick victory. They were running out of patience with Joe's cautious approach to battle. The criticisms against him grew stronger and stronger.

In July 1864, while Joe was planning his next attack on General Sherman at Peachtree Creek, he received a telegram from President Davis. The telegram ordered him to turn his troops over to General John B. Hood. "[Y]ou are hereby relieved from command," it read, meaning that Joe had been fired.

These ruins in Columbia, South Carolina, were typical of the devastation in the South.

The Surrender
of Tennessee

Joe Johnston was a quiet, gentle man whose temper sometimes startled the people around him. He could get furiously angry, shouting violent threats or galloping off on his horse at reckless speeds. Joe almost always calmed down within a few hours. He then thoroughly apologized to anyone he had offended with his outburst.

When Joe got the news that he had been fired, his response surprised everyone who knew him well. He had been feuding with Jefferson Davis for years, but this time Joe did not react in anger. He did not send a letter of protest or try to rally his supporters against Davis. He calmly accepted the decision and prepared to leave his command. Joe graciously met with General Hood to inform him of the status of the troops and the plans they had already put into action. He wrote a farewell address to his beloved Army of Tennessee, praising them for their hard work and bravery. "No longer your leader, I will watch your career, and will rejoice in your victories," he wrote.

That same evening, Joe Johnston rode quietly out of the camp. Some of the soldiers had heard what had happened. They ran to line the road, waving and cheering for their old general. When the rest of the troops found out that Joe had been dismissed, they reacted in shock and anger. They didn't know what they would do without "Old Joe." Many soldiers wrote home to their families expressing their distress at the loss of their leader. There was such a disturbance in the camp that the officers had to meet to discuss the best way to calm everyone.

For the next few months, Joe went home to Macon, Georgia, where he and Lydia lived. His friends received him warmly and gave him a hero's welcome.

Meanwhile, Joe's replacement wasted no time in attacking the Union forces. Just after Joe's departure, General Hood struck Sherman's army at Peachtree Creek. Two days later he attacked again, near Atlanta. Neither battle ended in victory, and more than 12,000 Confederate soldiers had lost their lives. Within a week, Hood launched his third battle—and failed again. This time he lost 5,000 men. Eventually, General Sherman's troops drove Hood to retreat to Alabama.

Hood made terrible decisions on the battlefield and was a poor planner. Twice more, General Hood led the Army of Tennessee into battle against General Sherman. He was defeated both times. At the battle near Franklin, the Confederates lost another 6,000 men. Six of their generals died in one day. By the time it was all over,

Hood had only managed to wipe out his own army. General Sherman easily captured Atlanta.

Back at his home in Macon, Joe followed the news and grew more alarmed with every report. He worried about his men and the state of the Confederate forces. He became sick with shingles, a virus that is triggered by stress or anxiety. There was nothing that Joe could do, but watch and wait. He hated feeling helpless.

As the situation grew worse and worse, the Confederate government lost confidence in their president. They voted to make Robert E. Lee the "general in chief," giving him full power to act without consulting President Jefferson Davis. Fifteen members of congress met with Lee, asking him to reappoint Joe to the command of the Tennessee Army. Over Jefferson Davis's strong objections, Lee did so.

Tennessee's soldiers had wrote a song about the disastrous efforts of General Hood and their wish for Joe's return. They sang it to the tune of the "Yellow Rose of Texas": "So now I'm marching southward; My heart is full of woe. I'm going back to Georgia to see my Uncle Joe. You may talk about your Beauregard and sing of General Lee, But the Gallant Hood of Texas played hell in Tennessee."

At first, Joe was reluctant to return. He feared that the situation was already beyond hope. He had discovered that some of the other generals had actively schemed behind his back to push him out of the army earlier. He didn't want to come back, only to be made a scapegoat, if the South lost the war. Joe's friends convinced him that Lee's offer was sincere. He was not being set up to take a fall. The army needed him.

Although they had been close friends in school, Joe Johnston and Robert E. Lee had grown apart. They hadn't spoken to each other since the Battle of Seven Pines, when Lee took over Joe's command. Joe struggled with jealousy over Lee's success. But when he heard that Lee himself had reappointed Joe to command the Army of Tennessee, all hard feelings were forgotten. Joe wrote about Lee to a friend, "In youth and early manhood I loved and admired him more than any man in the world . . . . Be assured that Knight of old never fought under his King more loyally than I'll serve under General Lee."

In February 1865 more than six months after he had been fired, Joe assumed command of the Army of Tennessee once again. Just as before, he found himself doing a lot of repair work. He restored order to the camp, smoothed over arguments between officers, and started gathering fresh supplies for the troops. A few weeks later, he led them into battle for the last time.

Joe's men were heavily outnumbered and still recovering from their losses under General Hood. Still, they bravely ambushed the Union forces at Bentonville, North Carolina. There was no clear-cut winner in the conflict, but the South claimed it as a victory. They had fought hard all day, inflicting serious damage on the Northern armies. Joe's men had not retreated under fire— they had driven the Union forces to retreat. Little ground had really been gained, but the soldiers' spirits soared. At a time when they had faced one defeat after another, this battle restored their hope. They felt they had proven that they could still fight and that the war wasn't over yet.

Confederate General Robert E. Lee surrendered the Army of Northern Virginia to Union general Ulysses S. Grant at Appomattox Court House, Virginia, ending the Civil War.

But, their joy did not last long. News came that General Robert E. Lee had been forced to surrender to General Ulysses S. Grant at Appomattox Court House on April 9, 1865. The war was over after all. Reluctantly, Jefferson Davis directed Joe to meet with General Sherman to

Joe Johnston and General Sherman first met to discuss Tennessee's surrender on April 17, 1865. As soon as they were alone, Sherman passed Joe a telegram he had just received. With great sadness, Joe read that President Abraham Lincoln had been assassinated. In sincerity, he told Sherman that Lincoln's death was "the greatest possible calamity" for the South. The nation needed President Lincoln's compassionate leadership. Without it, reconciliation between the North and the South would be a difficult and painful process.

discuss Tennessee's surrender. The two men met face-to-face for the first time in Durham, North Carolina. Both men were polite and cooperative. The tone of their meetings was serious, but not hostile. After several meetings and discussions with their superiors, they agreed on terms. On April 26, 1865, Joe Johnston officially surrendered the Army of Tennessee to the Union forces under the command of General William Tecumseh Sherman. And on May 2, 1865, Joe said his final goodbye to the army. In his last official order, he wrote to his men: "I shall always remember with pride the loyal support and generous confidence you have given me. I now part with you with deep regret, and bid you farewell with feelings of cordial friendship and with earnest wishes that you may have hereafter all the prosperity and happiness to be found in the world."

Union Civil War hero Ulysses S. Grant became the 18th president, serving from 1869 to 1877.

After the War

6

The Civil War lasted four long years. Those years were filled with misery and suffering as the country was torn apart. Families were divided, friendships were destroyed, and thousands and thousands of lives were lost. And now that it had ended, it was time to heal and rebuild. The process would take many years.

After the war, the Johnstons' first priority was Lydia's health. Throughout their marriage, Lydia had struggled with one illness after another. With Joe no longer in the military, the couple traveled together in search of a climate that would help improve Lydia's condition. They visited friends and family across the country and eventually settled in Virginia. To support himself, Joe took a job as president of a small railroad company. When the company failed, he accepted a position in the insurance business. By 1868, Joe had started his own insurance business—Joseph E. Johnston & Company. Joe invited some former Confederate officers to join him, and the business grew to be extremely successful.

With his financial needs met, Joe turned his attention to writing his memoirs. Many of the military leaders from both the North and the South had published their own accounts of the Civil War. In some cases, the books ended up being just an extension of the war itself—a kind of "Battle of the Books." Former generals and politicians took verbal shots at one another as they criticized each others' actions and defended their own. Joe became a leading participant in this battle. Often, he was described with great respect and given high praise in the autobiographies of his opponents. Union Generals Ulysses S. Grant and William Tecumseh Sherman both gave Joe credit for his military skills and the superior strategy he had used against them. Some of the officers on his own side were less complimentary. In fact, several books had already been published by Confederate generals who described Joe as lacking in talent and the ability to lead. He was deeply insulted.

Throughout the war, Joe felt that he had been misrepresented, misunderstood, and unfairly criticized. He thought that writing a book would give him a chance to explain his side of the story. Joe went to great lengths to write what he thought was an accurate version of the events that took place during the war. But the more Joe tried to defend himself, the worse he sounded. In his book, Joe came across as petty, resentful, and bitter. It didn't reflect the kind,

William Tecumseh Sherman died in February 1891. Joe Johnston served as one of his pallbearers. The funeral was held on a cold and rainy day. Joe stood beside the grave with his hat in his hands. Someone suggested that he put on his hat, so that he wouldn't get sick. Joe insisted on showing his old adversary the proper respect. "If I were in his place and he were standing here in mine, he would not put on his hat," Joe said. Joe did, in fact, catch a cold that day. His health quickly declined, and a few weeks after Sherman's funeral, Joe died.

Shown here are the covers from a series of biographies on Union Civil War leaders. Joe spent his later years working on his memoirs so that he could defend his reputation and present his version of events that took place during the war.

gracious, and humble man he was capable of being. When *Narrative of Military Operatives Directed During the Late War Between the States* was published in 1874, it didn't sell very well. Critics said that the book was nothing more than a lengthy attack on Jefferson Davis. The book's failure only added to Joe's long list of disappointments.

For the remainder of his life, Joe continued his feud with Davis through books, newspaper articles, and public comments. His friends begged him to let go of the past. For some reason, he just couldn't do it. Until the day he died, Joe was still trying to defend his reputation, still trying to prove that he had been right all along.

Even though he was no longer in the military, Joe found new ways to serve his country. In 1878, Joe was elected to the United States House of Representatives as the representative from Virginia. He served in Congress on the Military Affairs Committee. Later, Joe held a cabinet position in the administration of President

Grover Cleveland. He was appointed as Federal Railroad Commissioner.

Lydia's health never improved. Joe was devastated when she died at the age of 65, in 1887. He missed her terribly. Unlike Lydia, Joe had been blessed with unusually good health. Even as an old man, he had plenty of energy and enthusiasm. He worked hard right up until his retirement in 1889. Joe lived longer than many of his peers. He helped carry the caskets at the funerals of his old Union foes, Ulysses S. Grant, George McClellan, and William Tecumseh Sherman. Whenever he got the chance, Joe loved to visit other Civil War veterans and talk about old times.

On March 21, 1891, Joe died at the age of 84. He was buried in Baltimore, Maryland, next to Lydia and her family. At his funeral, hundreds of people came to pay their respects. Joe had not been a perfect man. He made his share of mistakes. Historians would argue for another hundred years over whether or not Joe deserved to be called a "great" general. But no one could question his loyalty to his country or his love for his troops. Joe Johnston had always dreamed of being a soldier and he served his country proudly to the very end.

GLOSSARY

artillery–the part of the army that uses large, powerful guns.

cadet–a young person being trained to serve in the military.

Civil War–the armed conflict between the North and South in the United States from 1861 to 1865.

Confederate States of America–the states that left the Unites States to form an independent nation; the South.

demerit–a mark against someone for doing something wrong.

dictate–to talk while someone else writes down your words.

furlough–time off from duty for people in the military.

frontier–the wilderness at the edge of a country.

memoirs–an autobiography, the story of a person's life.

plantation–a large farm.

regiment–a military unit.

reinforcements–extra troops sent in to strengthen a fighting force.

rival–a person who competes against another person.

secede–to formally withdraw from a group or organization.

slavery–the system in which someone is owned by another person and thought of as property.

strategy–a plan of attack.

tactics–methods for winning a battle.

topographical–describing the physical features of an area, such as rivers, valleys, and hills.

treaty–a formal agreement.

Union–the states that remained part of the Unites States during the Civil War; the North.

CHRONOLOGY

1807	Born Joseph Eggleston Johnston on February 3 in Farmville, Virginia.
1825	Enters United States Military Academy at West Point, New York.
1829	Graduates from West Point Military Academy.
1832	Serves in the Black Hawk War.
1835	Serves as an aide to General Winfield Scott in the Florida Seminole War.
1837	Resigns from the army to become an engineer.
1838	Reenters the army as a member of the Engineer Corps.
1845	Marries Lydia McLane on July 10 in Baltimore, Maryland.
1846	Fights in the Mexcian-American War; wounded three times.
1860	Promoted to brigadier general.
1861	Resigns from the U.S. Army to join the Confederate forces; appointed a full general by President Jefferson Davis. The Civil War begins.
1862	Attacks Union General George McClellan near Richmond; wounded in the Battle of Seven Pines.
1863	Appointed Commander of the Army of Tennessee.
1864	Engages in a lengthy strategic conflict with General William Tecumseh Sherman; removed from his command by President Jefferson Davis.

1865	Reappointed by Robert E. Lee as Commander of the Tennessee Army; surrenders to General Sherman on April 26. The Civil War ends.
1868	Starts his own insurance business, Joseph E. Johnston & Company.
1874	Publishes autobiography, *Narrative of Military Operations Directed During the Late War Between t he States.*
1878	Elected to the U.S. House of Representatives.
1891	Dies on March 21 in Baltimore, Maryland.

CIVIL WAR TIME LINE

1860   Abraham Lincoln is elected president of the United States on November 6. During the next few months, Southern states begin to break away from the Union.

1861   On April 12, the Confederates attack Fort Sumter, South Carolina, and the Civil War begins. Union forces are defeated in Virginia at the First Battle of Bull Run (First Manassas) on July 21 and withdraw to Washington, D.C.

1862   Robert E. Lee is placed in command of the main Confederate army in Virginia in June. Lee defeats the Army of the Potomac at the Second Battle of Bull Run (Second Manassas) in Virginia on August 29–30. On September 17, Union general George B. McClellan turns back Lee's first invasion of the North at Antietam Creek near Sharpsburg, Maryland. It is the bloodiest day of the war.

1863   On January 1, President Lincoln issues the Emancipation Proclamation, freeing slaves in Southern states. Between May 1–6, Lee wins an important victory at Chancellorsville, but key Southern commander Thomas J. "Stonewall" Jackson dies from wounds. In June, Union forces hold the city of Vicksburg, Mississippi, under siege. The people of Vicksburg surrender on July 4. Lee's second invasion of the North during July 1–3 is decisively turned back at Gettysburg, Pennsylvania.

1864 General Grant is made supreme Union commander on March 9. Following a series of costly battles, on June 19 Grant successfully encircles Lee's troops in Petersburg, Virginia. A siege of the town lasts nearly a year.

Union general William Sherman captures Atlanta on September 2 and begins the "March to the Sea," a campaign of destruction across Georgia and South Carolina. On November 8, Abraham Lincoln wins reelection as president.

1865 On April 2, Petersburg, Virginia, falls to the Union. Lee attempts to reach Confederate forces in North Carolina but is gradually surrounded by Union troops. Lee surrenders to Grant on April 9 at Appomattox, Virginia, ending the war. Abraham Lincoln is assassinated by John Wilkes Booth on April 14.

FURTHER READING

Egger-Bovet, Howard and Marlene Smith-Baranzini. *Book of the American Civil War.* New York: Little, Brown & Co., 1998.

Herbert, Janice. *The Civil War for Kids: A History with 21 Activities.* Chicago: Chicago Review Press, 1999.

Moore, Kay. *If You Lived at the Time of the Civil War.* New York: Scholastic, Inc., 1994.

Savage, Douglas J. *The Soldier's Life in the Civil War.* Philadelphia: Chelsea House Publishers, 2000.

Stanchak, John E. *Civil War.* New York: Dorling Kindersley Publishing, 2000.

PICTURE CREDITS

page

3: National Archives at College Park

6: National Archives at College Park

11: © JW Petty/Corbis

14: Painting by John F. Clymer c. 1845
HultonArchive by Getty Images

17: HultonArchive by Getty Images

19: Bettmann/Corbis

24: Corbis

26: Bettmann/Corbis

28: © Matthew B. Brady/Corbis

34: Bettmann/Corbis

36: National Archives at College Park

39: National Archives at College Park

42: Bettmann/Corbis

48: National Archives at College Park

50: HultonArchive by Getty Images

52: HultonArchive by Getty Images

59: Corbis

62: Lyndon Baines Johnson Library Austin, TX/National Archives

66: HultonArchive by Getty Images

Cover photo: National Archives at College Park

INDEX

Note: **Boldface** numbers indicate illustrations.

INDEX

ABOUT THE AUTHOR

CHRISTIN DITCHFIELD is an author, conference speaker, and host of the nationally syndicated radio program, *Take It To Heart!* She has interviewed celebrity athletes such as gymnast Mary Lou Retton, NASCAR's Jeff Gordon, tennis pro Michael Chang, the NBA's David Robinson, and soccer great Michelle Akers. Her articles have been featured in magazines all over the world.

A former elementary school teacher, Christin has written more than a dozen books for children on a wide range of topics—including sports, science, and history. She recently wrote a young adult biography of Martina Hingis for Chelsea House Publishers. Ms. Ditchfield makes her home in Sarasota, Florida.